'You're not from round here,
are you?'

'You're not from round here, are you?'
An A – Z of Proper People
and People from Off

by Roger Kite

Logaston Press

LOGASTON PRESS
Little Logaston Woonton Almeley
Herefordshire HR3 6QH
logastonpress.co.uk

First published by Logaston Press 2008
Reprinted 2012
Copyright © Roger Kite 2008
The Author asserts his moral right to be identified
as the author of this work

ISBN 978 1 906663 03 2

Typeset by Logaston Press
and printed in Great Britain by
Bell & Bain Ltd., Glasgow

A Little Something for Jan

An Introduction – of sorts

First, a confession: you're probably expecting this introduction to tell you what the book is going to be about. A reasonable expectation, after all. Well, sorry to disappoint you. All I will tell you instead is that the book is not what it seems, for what it seems to be about is not what it's really about. There are the lines of text to read, of course, but much more important is to read between the lines, to go from text to sub-text.

It's not what is in the book that matters, but what it points to. Its real subject lies elsewhere, well beyond the page, located in many times and places, appearing in many guises, is dark, troublesome, divisive, notoriously difficult to eradicate, and touches us all. Oddly enough, it often touches most those who feel sure they are immune to it.

Of course I could save you time and effort – and probably not a little irritation – by coming clean and simply telling you here and now what it's really about, and by now you're probably hoping that's exactly what I'll do. But no, that would defeat the point of the book. The whole point of the book, you see, is to encourage you, the reader, to fathom out for yourself what it's actually about, and in so doing to give some thought to its underlying subject-matter, and to see where you stand.

But perhaps a clue is justified. It might help you to know that although the book is meant to be funny at surface level, what it's really about is far from funny. In fact, it's so unfunny and of such seriousness and consequence that I can only approach the subject indirectly, through the medium of humour.

So now I've already told you a number of things about this book and I've told you these things rather grudgingly because in the world of comedy it is said that to have to explain a joke is to admit it's a poor joke to start with. Not that this book is a joke; it's more akin to a parable. But that's quite enough by way of clues ...

Starting off

There are some words you just have to feel sorry for. They seem harmless enough, giving years of faithful service tucked away in a dictionary, causing nobody any harm. Yet now and again they go off the rails, get into bad company, take on a whole new character and become a very different kettle of fish.

One such is 'off'. What a miserable little word this is. It has such a grim life and such negative overtones that you want to form a society to protect it: Off-Watch perhaps.

We are told to CLEAR OFF, SHOVE OFF, PUSH OFF, and much worse. We notice that the milk has GONE OFF, that we're FEELING a bit OFF, that we're generally having an OFF DAY. And we didn't think much of the remark: it was a BIT OFF. OFF-HAND even. The player was OFF-SIDE and we're GOING OFF the whole idea.

To add to this sad list we find that off, as well as being some kind of negative state, is surprisingly also a place. Not so much a place where people live now, but a place where people used to live, where they have come from. 'He's FROM OFF you know'. 'The family have lived here for five hundred years but, of course, they're really FROM OFF'.

There are many ways of putting people into pigeon-holes, of course. We can use social class, colour, religion, political views, ethnicity, how they speak, and so on. It's almost as complicated as it is boring and pointless. What we need is a system that's simple and that everyone will find easy to use: which is where my farmer friend comes in handy. She saves us all a lot of trouble by dividing humanity neatly and uncompromisingly into two clear-cut groups: people from off and what she defiantly calls 'proper' people. Now what could be simpler? And no one could take objection to such a division, surely?

There is a rich vocabulary for people from off: they are known as 'blow-ins' in Ireland, 'emmets' in Cornwall, 'grockels' in Devon, while proper people in France – although some authorities on the subject regard this as a contradiction in terms – make a distinction between *les gens d'ici* and *les gens d'ailleurs*. All of these are designed to separate local people from the rest of the world's population.

It goes without saying that as far as my farmer friend is concerned, proper people are primarily farmers or involved somehow or other in agriculture and food production, and have been so for generations. It also goes without saying that they are country dwellers and not townies, are locals and not incomers, and most importantly are locals to *her* locality. Surely no view could be more reasonable?

She realizes that on this definition proper people are likely to be found all over the place such as Oxfordshire, Lancashire, the Outer Hebrides, and so forth – but thinks that there are degrees of properness which in its purest form is to found *only* where *she* lives. Again, a perfectly reasonable point of view we can all take on board.

Those of a philosophical frame of mind, however, might want to ask a few questions, in the interests of clarification.

For instance, exactly how far away is off? Someone originating in Saudi Arabia or Poland or Iceland or Australia is obviously from off, but so apparently is someone from France, our nearest geographical neighbour. No problem so far. This seems straightforward until we consider the case of someone from a distant part of the UK, miles away from where *you* live – Carlisle or Penzance, for example. Are *they* from off? Well, of course they are. We mustn't make the problem more difficult than it really is. But what about someone from the next county, or even the next village? Again, no problem: they're from off.

It would seem then that distance has nothing to do with offness. What makes people from off is that they are not from where *she* is, or where *you* are. Despite any superficial similarities, they are different. You are normal: they are not.

However, the problem is more complicated yet, because there are people who live exactly where you live, maybe close neighbours, but who are nonetheless still from off. They have moved into the area, perhaps recently, perhaps centuries ago. They're still from off.

Also, another question comes to mind, bordering on the metaphysical: can someone who is from off somehow *become a* proper person, and if so, how? And how long might it take? How would you know the process had been completed? Can it in fact ever be achieved? Furthermore, do people from off *look* different from proper people? This is not an unknown suggestion.

Also worth considering is the possibility, admittedly bizarre, that a proper person might wish to become *like* a person from off.

Obviously such a fantasy would have to be carefully concealed. So in the interests of clarification we might want to know how exactly one can 'spot' a person from off? What are the tell-tale signs?

Perhaps it has to do with their appearance, or what they eat, or wear, or what sort of vehicle they drive. Perhaps it has to do with their patterns of speech and the words they actually use. Or more importantly with their values and beliefs.

To find out more about this complex subject you could, of course, go to university and take a degree in sociology. Although this would probably help it would be boring beyond belief and much more importantly, if you are a proper person, would stop you earning money for a year or two, something you would find deeply depressing. It would also involve you mixing with countless people from off, which it goes without saying is to be avoided at all cost.

Fortunately a much better solution is at hand, and at a fraction of the cost of going to college. Which is where this little dictionary comes into its own. It offers a comprehensive A-Z checklist of the give-away signs of offness, or offitude, or offery, not of course that it is needed by proper people since they know instinctively who is from off and who isn't, thereby suggesting that the process of becoming completely proper – known in the trade as 'properization' – is, after all, impossible to achieve. So this little guide-book-cum-dictionary is intended rather for the general reader. The title 'Know Your Grockel' came to mind, but was rejected on the grounds that only people in Cornwall would understand it.

Several kind people, all of them proper, have helped with this dictionary and I would like to mention them by name, but they seem a touch nervous. Since several of them are close friends I have reluctantly been obliged to accept their offers of huge sums of money to keep their identities secret. It's the least I can do.

So now for the dictionary ...

A is for Artichoke

People from off eat artichokes. Proper people do not, though they might know what they are.

Of course artichokes are not unique among vegetables as a means of separating proper people from people from off. Any dish containing Samos spinach, or Azur Star kohlrabi, or a Blue Hubbard squash, will certainly not have been made by a proper person.

Also, proper people strongly dislike having their food – to use a technical term – 'messed about'. They like it plain. They do not want their sprouts simmered for seven minutes in a *jus* of langoustines; they want them boiled for a couple of hours and plenty of them.

What they want is something tasty like mother used to make. They also require the hernia-producing quantities mother used to make. Mother after all could never have been accused of being a lightweight, in any sense of the word. Any woman capable of picking up two bales of straw at a time, while also smoking a pipe, would have given *nouvelle cuisine* a pretty wide berth.

In these progressive times, however, it is possible that some proper people will indeed have heard of *nouvelle cuisine*. The mere detail of not knowing what it is mustn't stop you from rejecting it. All you need to know is that it's French and so is definitely out.

A further sure-fire culinary litmus test concerns the revealing subject of sauces. Any proper person will recognize a number of tried-and-tested sauces: brown sauce, mint sauce, parsley sauce, bread sauce, and tomato sauce. Possibly, in these permissive days, tartare sauce. Though for sure, not *sauce tartare*. Obviously foreign.

B is for Baler Twine

People from off carry all manner of things in their pockets: the latest model of mobile phone, SAT NAV equipment, miniature computers, and for foggy days, Fisherman's Friends. Proper people carry the Farmer's Friend, otherwise known as baler twine. This has a wide range of purposes nothing to do with baling: to create makeshift halters for leading horses, to hold up trousers, and most useful of all, to secure gates which would otherwise be used by people from off to gain access to something called a 'Public Right of Way' [see **Public Rights of Way**].

B is for Best Clothes

This is a particularly reliable thing to observe: people from off put on what they call 'casuals' at the weekend.

Proper people on the other hand save the weekends for putting on their best outfits. The only occasions mid-week when they will wear their best are funerals and agricultural shows.

At market, or when visiting the bank, the oldest clothes possible will be worn. Wealth should not be advertised.

$\mathcal{B}$ is for Brussels

Proper people regard Brussels as both a boon and a curse. They can't live with it and they can't live without it.

People from off, on the other hand, think of Brussels as something you buy by the pound, boil for twenty-seven seconds and serve in a *sauce à l'ail à la Provençale*.

C is for Carwash

Proper people never wash their vehicles except on two occasions [see also **4-Wheel Drives**] whereas people from off regularly pamper their cars, washing, shampooing, polishing, and waxing them.

They usually do these things in a prominent position, where neighbours can observe their antics. (Proper people, by the way, are never observed, since their nearest neighbours are probably half a mile away, at the next farm.) The more expensive the car, the more often it gets valeted. People from off even take their car to a carwash. Proper people have heard of such places but have no intention of ever visiting one.

C is for Chickens

Proper people, unlike people from off, do not keep chickens: they keep hens or, better still, fowls. And unlike people from off they certainly do not keep fancy hens.

The same observation applies to other fancy animals: ponies, dogs, cats, sheep, etc. It applies also to fancy food and first names.

C is for The Council

People from off work assiduously to get on the council. They get on to committees, seek election as officers, and make a name for themselves, not to mention a nuisance.

Proper people, by contrast, are so to speak *naturally* on the council. There is a being-on-the-council gene which they have by the bucketful.

D is for Dogs

A dog from off will be on a lead. It will probably have a collar and a name tag. It might even have a tartan coat for use in cold weather. People from off have dogs as companions, and call them silly names, like Mr. Wilkinson, or Jeeves, or Genevieve, instead of Bob, Floss, Fly, Tess, or Lad – proper names for the proper dogs of proper people.

It goes without saying that proper people never have their dogs on leads. They do not own a lead. Their dogs are dogs with a purpose. They work sheep, catch rabbits, and retrieve pheasants during the shoot. Occasionally people from off take their dogs off their lead – at which point if they annoy sheep they are shot by proper people – the dogs, not the people, that is.

$\mathcal{D}$ is for Doing Things

A common complaint from proper people about people from off is that they simply don't know how to *do* things. Now clearly there are lots of things they do know how to do, such as managing off-shore investments or knowing which golf club to use. So what are proper people getting at?

What they mean is that your typical person from off is of no use to them at all: he has no idea how to build a fence, trouse a hedge, deliver a calf, work a sheepdog, worm a horse, hang a gate, or do anything else remotely useful to a proper person. So, grim though it is, the question has to be asked: just what are people from off *for*?

E is for Elderly

Proper people who are elderly
or old never, but never, give up.
They go on to the bitter end. Basing
their behaviour on that of royalty,
they never hand over to the next
generation until it is unavoidable.
Consequently they never retire,
for even when they have actually
finished running the farm they are
still there, and are consulted on a
regular basis, usually about tax-
avoidance.

The elderly from off, by
contrast, probably took early
retirement at 50, unless they
could fix it earlier. They think of
themselves as retired, which
means they can now
embark on a life of
endless golf, cruises,
supper-parties and
worming their way
onto the council.

E is for The Electric

      People from off simply cannot imagine life without electricity. Proper people on the other hand can remember life *before* electricity. If old enough they can probably remember times before running water. But best of all, they can also remember times before people from off.

Æ is for The Environment

People from off bang on endlessly about the
environment – how to protect it, save it, treat it with
respect, be at one with it, and so on. Mysteriously
however, proper people know that they *are* the
environment.

$\mathcal{F}$ is for 4-Wheel Drives

Since both proper people and people from off have these, a little care must be exercised in using them for identification purposes. The main point to remember is that the two groups use them for completely different things. Proper people carry sheep in them, or bales of hay, or fencing-posts and wire-netting.

And, of course, never clean them, except on the day before they plan to sell the vehicle for another model. Or the day before attending a funeral, providing the funeral is going to come complete with decent refreshments.

A clean 4-wheel drive is the acid test that people from off are its owners. Owners from off use them for off-roading, which is not at all the same thing as a proper person taking his 4-wheel drive across the fields to mend a fence or to attend to a sick cow.

Off-roading is generally not approved of by proper people, unless it takes place on *their* land, in which case the prospect of money changing hands helps them see the activity in a brand new light.

Also, people from off go on holiday in their 4-wheel drives. You see them lined up at ferry terminals, with building materials to do up the house they have just bought in Provence or Tuscany.

Proper people look forward to summer holidays, because at this time hordes of people from off go abroad which is considered by proper people to be a very good thing.

G is for Gardens

If someone spends serious money on a garden, or even claims to have a garden at all, he's certainly from off. No question. Foolproof test.

Proper people do not have gardens. They have a bit of land in front of the farmhouse but this has nothing in common with a garden and must not be confused with a garden. It has only one function: it is where rusting tractors are laid to rest. And old combines, and baling machines. And dead animals. Mountains of rusting machinery are considered a good thing by proper people since they tend to decrease the chances of adjacent land being bought by someone from off.

G is for Glats

A further sure-fire test to identify the person from off would be to ask if they have glats. If they ask what kind of disease this is, or if it's catching, they're from off.

Glat: a gap in a hedge, normally filled in with rusty tractor parts and old bedsteads.

G is for Gorse

Proper people know that once a year the remains of the gorse must be burned, to allow the underlying grass shoots to get going for next year. Not only is this necessary it's also enjoyable, a pleasant part of the rural calendar. People from off, agitated that the smoke might discolour their washing, or leave sooty traces on the newly manicured car, call the fire-brigade.

As a matter of fact, proper people get real pleasure from all kinds of activities involving fire, from having proper fires in their homes, to piling up and then burning enormous mountains of trouse following hedging or fencing work, together with a few old tractor tyres.

Having made sure that the wind will blow the huge clouds of acrid smoke away from *their* property, they genuinely hope that the family from off, who live in the cottage along the lane and who, with several small children, always have washing on the line, won't mind too much.

$\mathcal{H}$ is for Holidays

People from off regularly go on holiday, at least once a year. The more off they are, the further and more often they go. You can measure offness by air miles.

Proper people, of course, never go on holiday, though they do travel. This apparent contradiction is easily explained: they might go to France, or New Zealand – but only to compare notes on lambing techniques, or artificial insemination. Also this kind of travel is always free: it has been paid for by some organisation or other, but certainly not by the proper person. This is explained by the innate understanding of proper people that money is not for spending [see **Money**].

H is for Houses

People from off spend much time and money upgrading their houses, either by regularly moving to a better property, or by home improvements. They knock walls out to make through-rooms, they put in en-suite bathrooms, they construct patios, decking and garden rooms. Their houses glow with pride.

Proper people, on the other hand, don't have houses, they just live in the accommodation that goes with the farm. When a farm comes up for sale, what normally happens is that the farmer will make a thorough inspection of the land, out-buildings, etc, but show no interest whatever in the house. That's no concern of his. It's his wife's domain, together with the B&B business, and the hens [see **Chickens**].

I is for Income Tax

Those from off quite like paying income tax. It's a reflection of their status in life. Proper people, by contrast, will move heaven and earth to avoid paying any income tax, or as little as possible [see **Money**].

For a proper person to admit to paying a lot of tax is a shameful thing, akin to cruelty to animals or children.

ℐ is for Indignation

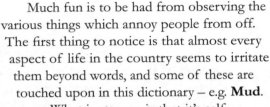

Much fun is to be had from observing the various things which annoy people from off. The first thing to notice is that almost every aspect of life in the country seems to irritate them beyond words, and some of these are touched upon in this dictionary – e.g. **Mud**.

What is strange is that it's self-inflicted and ever so easily remedied.

Naturally no proper person would be impolite or unfeeling enough ever to make such a suggestion. It's just a thought, but a thought that frequently comes into the mind of a proper person.

So what are the things that drive them mad? Well, first, there's so much mud about. You can't even walk across a ploughed field – using the right of way, of course – without getting mud on your new £300 suede boots. And it doesn't stop there. It gets onto the car, and into the house. There ought to be a law to make mud illegal.

And rain. Why does it rain so much? And why does it rain at the very moment the guests are arriving for the barbecue? What has the MP got to say about it? It's nothing short of a disgrace.

Not to mention the smells. Everywhere you go you are assailed by smells of cows, sheep, silage and, worst of all, muck-spreading. Why can't farmers learn to keep things clean? We keep our cars clean, why can't they tidy up their animals a bit? And why can't they stop their cockerels from making such a racket in the early hours. It's not natural. Proper people delight in this free entertainment, *free* being one of their favourite words.

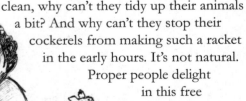

J is for Jumble Sale

Many people from off love jumble sales. It's not so much a question of what they *buy* from the sale as what they *take to* it. People from off regularly take their unwanted Rolex watches, their out of fashion hand-painted Royal Doulton tableware, and last month's digital camera.

Proper people on the other hand never contribute anything to jumble sales as they feel they 'must have something for it' and giving things away is not an idea they are at all familiar with.

$\mathcal{K}$ is for Kites

People from off are delighted that kites have been reintroduced in places and can be seen soaring in the skies. People from off are also fond of badgers, and even foxes, which they regard as cute. They have even been known to catch town foxes and bring them into the countryside, or worse still, keep them as pets. The thought of controlling the numbers of these predators appals them.

People from off at the same time bemoan the fact that ground-nesting birds, such as skylarks, have almost disappeared. It seems that people from off have an innate inability to put two and two together.

𝒦 is for Knowing

Proper people, when they meet, ask one another what they know. This is the correct form of address, to find out if someone has news to share, or unsubstantiated gossip to spread, etc.

People from off, because they either know nothing, or else think they know everything, do not use this form of address.

Proper people are naturally reticent even amongst themselves, but especially with people from off. They tell them very little, and, if questioned, nothing at all.

People from off sometimes attempt to 'get to know' proper people, or become their friends, or show they are totally fascinated by their life and work. But they invariably do this by asking the wrong questions – questions guaranteed to reveal their ignorance and to ensure that no information is revealed, such as: how many sheep do you have? How many acres? Do you employ many people? Or, worst of all, roughly how much do you earn a year?

Proper people as a rule have little contact with people from off. It's not that they consciously avoid them, it's just that their paths do not naturally cross, a situation made even more likely by ensuring that all gates, especially those at the entrance to something called a 'Right of Way', are kept constantly secured. This is something that makes a proper person very happy.

$\mathcal{L}$ is for Land

If you have land you're a proper person.
If you have a garden, even a massive garden,
you're from off. Simple.

$\mathcal{L}$ is for Limousine

A person from off frequently seeks to become the friend of a proper person. They do this by asking 'intelligent' questions [see **Knowing**], but invariably give themselves away by making revealing mistakes: 'You have a flock of limousines, don't you?' would be a typical example. Or, 'Are they chevrolets?'

An even more dangerous minefield to negotiate is the mass of words to do with sheep: tup, ram, ewe, hog, wether, etc. These are more or less guaranteed to show up the person from off.

The most alarming example of off-ignorance was provided by the woman who thought that cows were 'lady horses'.

M is for Money

Proper people know that money is quite obviously not for spending. This is not something they have learned, you understand. They were born knowing it. The knowledge has been passed from generation to generation in the genes.

People from off spend lots of money as a matter of course, whereas proper people are likely to spend money if and only if it leads to a considerable reduction in income tax.

M is for Mud

People from off tend to
get very hot and bothered about
mud, especially when it appears
in front of their houses, or
when it gets onto their cars
and clothes [see **Indignation**].
They write letters to the papers,
contact the local councillor,
bother their MP. They even
instigate legal proceedings.
Proper people on
the other hand have never
heard of mud and would
not even recognise it were
it pointed out to them.
It's an alien concept and as
such something visible *only* to
people from off.

$\mathcal{N}$ is for ... Yes

'No' is often proper-talk for 'yes'. For example, a proper person visiting might be invited to have a cup of tea. He would, of course, decline. He might do this more than once.

But if the host is a proper person too he will persevere, because he knows that 'No' really means 'Yes'. Eventually the guest will consider that the proper protocol has been observed for long enough, and might well ask if there are any biscuits.

For a proper person visiting a person from off this is a risky business. He will be asked if he wants a cup of tea. He declines, because this is what proper people do. And the person from off, totally failing to understand the language, will not repeat the offer, leaving the guest tea-less.

O is for Oak

People from off make collections of early oak furniture – a lovely joint stool, a bargain at only £7,500 from a delightful shop in the Cotswolds, and that Welsh dresser lovingly restored and the French oak farmhouse kitchen table shipped over from Brittany.

Proper people are not aware of having furniture, they just have the same old bits and pieces that have been in the family and in the same farmhouse for three hundred years. They are invariably priceless.

Where a little modernizing has been done, you can bet that the old stuff has definitely not been thrown out. It's simply been put into the attic, or the barn. The hens are probably living in it.

O is for Oonts

A person from off might well send for a proper
person to get rid of his oonts and their tumps. Clearly
it would need a proper person to do this since no one
from off would have the slightest idea how to go
about it. It's a foreign language to them. It's another
world.

Oonts, or wonts, are moles, whose little hills are known as tumps.

P is for Public Rights of Way

People from off go on endlessly about rights of way and public footpaths. They get angry when demarcated rights of way are inadvertently blocked, hidden or shared with dangerous cattle.

Proper people simply cannot understand this anger since they have never heard of rights of way and if they were shown one would not know what they were supposed to be looking at.

Q is for Quarrels

Both people from off and proper people have quarrels. People from off quarrel among themselves and with proper people, usually about mud, or subsidies, etc. Proper people never quarrel with people from off since they are reluctant to recognize their existence. They do however have quarrels amongst themselves. This is a reliable way of identifying a proper person: a good quarrel will usually last for several generations.

You know a really good quarrel when you meet one because it will have lasted so long there is no one left who has the faintest idea what the original quarrel was about. However, this is not a sufficient reason to abandon the quarrel. A good quarrel, like a good wine, matures with age. The children of the family are therefore instructed in how to keep the quarrel going into the next generation, like a precious family heirloom.

Q is for Quicks

Your typical person from off will, it goes without saying, have a garden. This will typically contain a pond, decking, a water feature, a piece of expensive abstract garden sculpture, garden lighting and a solar-powered croaking frog. The whole garden will be enclosed by a wooden fence, painted blue.

A proper person has no garden; his land is demarcated by planting quicks.

Quicks: hawthorn, planted to form a hedge.

Q is for Quid Pro Quo

Only people from off use foreign words and expressions. Thus, de facto, ad hoc and the like, are off limits. So are hoi polloi, ensemble, en-suite, entre nous, etc.

Even though times are changing, there are limits to what is acceptable in the language of proper people. *Tempora mutantur nos et in illis mutamur** – but not round here, thank you.

* Times change and we change with them.

R is for Ramblers

People from off, in particular those who ramble, complain endlessly about rights of way and public footpaths. They get steamed up whenever they are not signposted, are fenced, blocked, or otherwise rendered unusable. They join protest groups, organize marches and bother councillors and MPs.

Proper people simply cannot understand any of this since they have never heard of rights of way, on account of all the signs having been removed. Anyway in the final analysis if a person from off is convinced that there *is a* right of way across that field he is welcome to use it. He has only to take a machete to the metre-wide bramble hedge, use industrial bolt-cutters to deal with the barbed wire securing the gate, first making quite sure it is not electrified, and away he goes.

Meanwhile, he can be confident that the Welsh Black bull nonchalantly observing all of this probably couldn't care less. Well, fairly confident.

$\mathcal{R}$ is for Red

'Seeing red' means different things to a person from off and a proper person. To the former it is what happens when he spots mud on the road, or gets stuck for miles behind a tractor, whereas for the proper person it's something of which he much approves and which brings great joy into his life: red diesel.

R is for Rover

For a proper person it's a vehicle. Even better, it's a vehicle on which he doesn't have to pay VAT. What a shame he is not allowed to put red diesel in the tank, thereby making a further saving. For a person from off, Rover is the dog, but only if they are unable to come up with a less suitable name such as Montague or Mirabella.

A further difference is that people from off generally take better care of their Rovers than proper people take of their vehicles.

S is for School

For a person from off the school their children attend is something they agonize over. It ranks almost as important as regular holidays abroad and having a decent cleaning-lady, and is not far behind getting elected to the council. They have even been known to move house in order to ensure that their offspring get into a particular school.

Proper people, by contrast, have a rather different attitude towards schools. They see them as more or less worthwhile, but not particularly important to *their* children, whose careers are already clearly mapped out: they will join the family farm. End of worry.

S is for Sheep

People from off, once they have been living in the countryside for a year or two, can easily recognize a sheep when they see one and effortlessly distinguish it from a cow. Proper people on the other hand don't know about sheep in general: they only know about specific varieties – Kerries, Welsh Mountain, Blue-Faced Leicesters and so on.

S is for Snow

Many people from off love snow. Everything about it delights them. They spend fortunes to go on holidays to places where snow is to be found, having first checked with the travel agent that there is snow and that it's of the right sort. Winter sports beckon. Thus people from off climb up things, then slide down them. They have no fear of falling off things and breaking legs, since such people always have private medical insurance. People from off see snow as an opportunity to spend money, which they see as a good thing. Even better to *be seen* spending it.

Proper people, by contrast, thoroughly dislike snow. There is nothing about it which pleases them. There is a particular reason for this. Proper people, unlike people from off, like to know where their money is, and from time to time to be able to see it. Hence the problem with snow.

Snow, for proper people, is the same colour as their assets: sheep. So, in snow they can't easily see their assets and this unnerves them to the point of making them quite morose.

S is for Subsidies

Clearly, proper people are all for them. They look forward to them as eagerly as a tax rebate. People from off, by contrast, see them as a further example of fecklessness and unmerited favouritism.

$\mathcal{T}$ is for Tools

The tools you keep around you are a pretty good indicator of whether you are a person from off or a proper person. Another indicator is the place where tools are stored.

A person from off normally keeps tools in the garage. The proper person, of course, does not own such a thing, and certainly not one with doors, electric or otherwise. Proper people keep their vehicles in the farmyard, or the barn, or in some other makeshift out-building.

The person from off has lots of identifying paraphernalia in the garage: for instance, an electric lawnmower, an electric strimmer, electric hedge clippers. Proper people have no dealings with such objects. Nor with the dozens of partly-used tins of paint normally stored in the person from off's garage.

A proper person would only redecorate his farmhouse when it had been so neglected that the services of a professional decorator were needed – in which case the painter would provide and get rid of all the materials required to do the job.

T is for Tractor

Tractors serve many purposes: to get across fields, to pull and operate machinery, and to trim roadside hedges in the autumn. But tractors have one other important function, which endears them no end to proper people. They are an excellent and reliable irritant to people from off.

An experienced tractor driver, needless to say a proper person, can cause untold stress and annoyance to people from off. He knows how to drive sufficiently near the middle of the road to allow almost enough room for the seventeen cars behind to try to overtake. Almost enough room, but not quite.

And why drive at twenty-five miles an hour when you can drive at five miles an hour and enjoy not one but two advantages? Not only do you greatly annoy the people from off behind you, rushing to get to the golf course, or to a crucial hair appointment, but also you use less fuel [see R is for **Red**].

Another skill of the experienced tractor driver is to give the impression that he is about to pull into a lay-by, to allow cars to get by. At the very last moment he changes his mind. This is driving of a high order — and enormously rewarding.

T is for Tup

A person from off has no idea what this is.
It is one word from a wide range of vocabulary
which separates the proper person from someone
from off. Knowing what these terms mean is learned
early, along with learning to walk, and is as natural
as cutting one's first tooth. Total fluency in this
language is probably impossible for a person from off.
At least the proper person hopes so.

𝒰 is for Unusual First Names

This is a fire-proof indicator. It works every time. If you meet a Zoë, she's from off. You know this straight away because no proper person would dream of using a name which requires an accent. The whole idea is too pretentious for words. Similarly names such as François, Brünhilde, Eugénie, and Hélène are ruled out.

These names are off limits because they are clearly foreign. This is reasonable and to be expected. But it is not only foreign names that give the game away. Fancy names in general are unacceptable. The idea of finding a proper person called Sienna, or Chablisse, or Jonquil is too ridiculous.

Also proper people avoid names like Craig, Wayne and Brett. They just don't like them. It's not that proper people have anything against such names, which in the 70s were common – if you'll excuse the pun – it's just that these names don't suit proper people.

You know where you are with a Mary, Henry, William, or Janet. Nothing fancy. Thoroughly dependable. Safe as subsidies.

$\mathcal{V}$ is for Vegetarians

By and large, only people from off are vegetarians and proper people are suspicious of them. So a vegetarian is doubly suspect. Proper people, because their families have lived where they are for generations, can remember times when they were jolly lucky to see a piece of meat at all, except for rabbits. Now, like most proper people, they are involved in meat production. So it goes without saying that anyone *choosing* not to eat meat is considered ungrateful and frankly unnatural.

V is for Vegans

As for vegans, proper people might have heard of them, but only proper people interested in astronomy actually know which planet they come from.

W is for Weather

It has to be admitted that just about everyone talks about the weather. It's one of our national pastimes. People from off often get troubled by the weather, but always for reasons that mean absolutely nothing whatsoever to proper people.

For example: it's raining. It will stop the golf. And it means the car can't be washed and polished, even though it's been a whole week since it was last done. Whatever will the neighbours think?

Snow is a problem too. If there's not enough snow, or it's the wrong sort, the skiing trip to the Alps will have to be called off. And if it's too windy, people from off have problems getting their gas-fired barbeques to light. Fog too is a trial. The flight to Tuscany to see how their olive grove is doing will have been cancelled.

For proper people too the weather is all-important, but for proper reasons. It affects their work and livelihood, or, put another way, their money. Prolonged rain means the cattle will have to be moved to higher ground; strong winds and heavy rain mean the hens will go off laying, and snow means all sorts of trouble, especially during lambing [see S for **Snow**].

W is for Wind Turbines

Attitudes to these are a useful guide to identification. A proper person is definitely against wind turbines unless they're on his land and generating, in addition to electricity, a sizeable income.

People from off think that wind turbines, like nuclear power, will save the planet and are therefore a good thing. But for some obscure reason people from off prefer not to live near them.

Proper people too are keen on saving the planet, but realize that only they can do this.

X is for Xmas

People from off love Christmas. It presents them with a golden opportunity to indulge in two of their favourite occupations: spending money unnecessarily, and entertaining people they don't know and wouldn't like if they did.

For proper people, however, Christmas is a very different story. Certainly it's a time for the family to come together and celebrate the coming of another round of subsidies. But it also brings its own problems. Apart from heralding another tax year for some, it's also a time for working even harder and longer than normal since the usual paid help is temporarily unavailable: they are too busy with their own Christmas festivities to do a day's work.

For the proper person there is one other blight on the Christmas festivities, something guaranteed to dampen the feeling of goodwill to all men – and it's to do with postage stamps. There's an even chance that the proper person will receive Christmas cards from people from off, this being part of their ongoing attempt to ingratiate themselves with their proper neighbours

Now, as we have seen, the proper person dislikes spending money at all, but to have to fork out cash for the benefit of someone from off is likely to cast gloom over the whole proceedings.

X is for Xenophobia

Proper people are naturally friendly and so it's to be hoped that nothing contained in this modest dictionary gives the opposite impression. The bottom line is that proper people need other proper people. They simply could not survive without them. The hay has to be bought from somewhere, the horses have to be shod, the animals taken to market, and so on. Proper people, together with their various vital trades and professions, sustain the countryside. They *are* the countryside.

So what about people from off? Well, proper people consider them – how can I put this without giving offence? – as *extraneous* and a touch *dilettantish,* terms which the dictionary defines as 'not essential, coming from without, irrelevant, not belonging' and 'a person whose interest in a subject is superficial rather than professional'. Oh dear! Maybe if they got to know them better?

People from off, in turn, have fairly fixed views about proper people, referring to them as – how can I put this without giving offence? – close-knit, probably interbred, canny, much wealthier than their frequent protestations of poverty suggest, not too keen on formal education, well in with councillors, experts on tax avoidance, etc. Oh dear! Perhaps if people from off got to know them a little better?

Y is for Year

You could be forgiven for thinking that a year is a year: the same for everybody, proper people and people from off alike. You would be wrong.

For people from off, the year is marked out by events more or less unknown to proper people – the walking holiday in the Massif Centrale, the cruise around the Baltic, the watercolour course in Tuscany, swimming with dolphins in the Mediterranean, photographing polar bears, and so on. Even those events limited to this country will be equally alien to proper people: the start of Wimbledon, the opening of the Summer Exhibition at the National Gallery, the new production of an avant garde ballet in Birmingham, etc.

For proper people too the year is set on its way by special periods and dates, but all totally beyond the comprehension of people from off. Some of these have names that seem to come from distant times – Lady Day, Rogation Days, Candlemas, for example. Typical others might be the date of the annual ram sale at such and such a place, or the annual cob sale, which to the person from off would probably indicate some part of a food festival.

Z is for Zucchini

No further comment needed. You can work this one out for yourself.

A Conclusion – of sorts

Once again, you're probably expecting some kind of conclusion now that you've reached the end of the book: some kind of summing-up, a drawing together of strands, an overview. An explanation would be nice. A reasonable enough thing to ask. But once again I'm going to disappoint you and stick to the original plan, which was to encourage *you* to make your own interpretation, to ask your own questions.

Giving people the answers to questions they haven't asked is always a waste of time. And sometimes it's just as futile giving them answers to questions they *have* asked, because they are your answers, not theirs. No, the most I can wish for is that this little book – which, as you know, isn't about what it seems to be about – will help produce questions about a very important topic. Or several?